NO MORE EXCUSES...

it's time to be HER!

Charleston, SC
www.PalmettoPublishing.com

Hardcover ISBN: 979-8-8229-4527-2
Paperback ISBN: 979-8-8229-4528-9

NO MORE EXCUSES...

it's time to be HER!

Jo Scott

To my children, who continue to inspire me to become
the best version of myself daily for them.

To Tiger: even though you didn't receive the best version
of me, you paved the way for how love is supposed to be,
and those shoes will be hard to fill.

To my future husband: I will continue to pray, cover,
and uplift you, for you will receive the best version of myself.
I can't wait to share my life with you.

I love you all.

TABLE OF CONTENTS

Introduction 1

Chapter 1: How to Use 7

Chapter 2: Pros and Cons 13

Chapter 3: Dating Yourself 31

Chapter 4: Triggers 37

Chapter 5: Continue Dating Yourself 42

Chapter 6: Be Soft 58

Chapter 7: What's New 75

Chapter 8: Let's Talk 83

Chapter 9: Loving Yourself 90

Chapter 10: What's on Your Mind? 93

Chapter 11: You 96

Chapter 12: Escape 101

Chapter 13: Journaling 108

Chapter 14: What's Next? 163

Chapter 15: "Phenomenal Woman" 167

About the Author 170

Ask yourself this question:
Are you ready to fully enjoy
your new life
and feel at ease and secure
within yourself,
which you know you deserve?

INTRODUCTION

Congratulations! Today will be your first step toward *No More Excuses...* This is not a January 1 journal, not a "new year, new me" journal. This is a "new me, new life" journal, channeling thoughts and recognizing and dealing with possible overacted emotions, overthinking, anxiety, and self-doubt. Ask yourself these questions. Do you want to repeat the same actions? Are you ready to truly enjoy your new life and feel at ease and secure within yourself, which you know you deserve?

Regular journaling has been shown to reduce anxiety and stress. I don't know about you, but I have dealt with both plus depression, and more times than not, I came out with overactive negative thinking and emotions. Journaling will access the left side of your brain, which is the analytical and rational part; while the left side of your brain is being engaged, the right side will then be free to be creative. This will remove mental blocks and allow you to use all your brain capacity to better understand yourself, others, and your surrounding environment.

Journaling can create a positive impact on your life not only by allowing you to get your thoughts out on paper but also by using your physical senses—the head-to-body effect. You think and then you do. For example, God will give a pastor or preacher the message first; they are meant to be the "head" of the church, and through the "head," they will present it to the body—the people of the church.

You ought to be at a place that gives you serenity, either on your lounge chair on the back porch sipping some homemade lemonade...a dimmed light, the smell of coffee, the distant chatter of others, and the sound of soft jazz music playing at your local café or at the beach, letting the sun hit your skin, listening to the crashing of the waves, that soft breeze caressing your body—whatever or wherever brings the most peace to you.

Serenity Prayer

God, grant me the serenity to accept the things I cannot change,
the courage to change the things I can,
and the wisdom to know the difference.

—Reinhold Niebuhr

Breathe, exhale, and relax, then allow yourself time to reflect or collect your thoughts and emotions to let them flow from your mind to the pen then to the paper, slowing your mind down to focus on your thoughts and feelings—not only to focus but to rationalize and channel those thoughts and feelings.

How many of you can say "daaaang" after barely escaping your anxiety breakdown and sinking deeper into the rabbit hole? Even though you may have reacted on impulse instead of considering the facts that were presented in front of you to then make your final decision, thought, or action, you will be in tune with yourself, and by doing so, you will create positive well-being in your mental, social, and psychological health.

Story Time: I have been with my husband since I was nineteen years old. I was still young and hadn't experienced a lick of life yet. When we got married, my mind was set on being a good wife, working to take care of the household, and then becoming a mother. We were living life, but being married was like living in a bubble. I saw and heard about the outside world from other people, but I was not a part of it, because I was a wife, and by this time a mother, not a young, single twenty-year-old. You tend to act differently in your situation. You wouldn't act single if you're married. I never really experienced it because my focus was on my family and not what was happening on the "outside."

With this, I never took time to really learn myself, to get to know her. I asked myself, how do I like my eggs—sunny-side up, over easy, or scrambled? Do I even like eggs? I really didn't know. So you could imagine with a question as simple as this how separated I was from myself. I was focused so much on what was around me. I was the wife who put herself last. Well, my situation was a little different since my husband suffered from a chronic liver disease. He needed more than I did.

Although I was a young woman, I had to prioritize my role as a wife and mother rather than focusing on being a young woman in her twenties. I don't think I need to elaborate on the part where many people say, "The twenties are your prime years; do what you want in your twenties, then grow up in the thirties."

I never properly loved myself or learned how because I didn't see the importance of it at that time. I needed to be his wife and their mother. I thought that was how it was supposed to be. Yes, I do believe your spouse and children are a priority, but you are the ultimate priority. This is not being inconsiderate or selfish. If I don't take care of myself, how can I take care of anyone else?

Life continued. Baby one came, then two, then three, and finally, baby four. It is easy to slip into a routine and go about life, but you are just there going through the effects of it, not truly in it—living it or experiencing it. Picture this: you know the moon and stars are there. You know the birds and crickets are there. But when was the last time you stopped—literally stopped—to go outside and look at the moon's light, see the stars, hear the birds singing their songs, and really watch the clouds? This would be truly experiencing it, not just going through the effects of it.

After my husband's passing, I found myself falling; I didn't know who I was, and with this came countless tragic mistakes that caused heartbreak, mine included. I didn't see the value of me. I lost the love I knew was in me; it was buried deep, compacted with all this illusion of happiness, illusion of having it together, illusion that I was fine...*illusion*! I smiled, I laughed, and I put on my "representative," but with this I was dying inside, and no one knew.

Showing your representative simply means that you are giving the persona or image that you consciously or unconsciously project to others. It's typically polished, composed, and focused on highlighting your positive attributes while downplaying or concealing your flaws. However, not with malicious intent or deceitfulness, but rather to showcase your most admirable traits to garner favor and ultimately be well-regarded. You want to find the balance between presenting your representative self and embracing your full, flawed self is a nuanced process influenced by individual preferences, social norms, and relationship dynamics. While there's value in portraying confidence and competence, genuine connections thrive on authenticity and acceptance of each other's imperfections.

I didn't see me as God saw me. I was lost. I wanted to get out, get out of the hole I dug so deep for myself, but even wanting to get out, I felt like I couldn't. It felt like a hold was on me. Was it too late for me? My depression got deeper, stronger, and more powerful. I hurt the closest person to me, with now my regrets are high. My thoughts in my head told me, "It is what it is, and you can't get any better."

During this time, I got a tattoo on my arm that says in French, "I am beautiful, I am enough, make today count." I was screaming from the top of my lungs, *"Help me, please!"* But with shame, embarrassment, guilt, and regret, I hadn't known what to do or how to escape this hell that I had put myself in. It may seem so easy to say, but when your mind is so impacted by self-doubt, a lack of love for yourself, and confidence, you don't see any light at the end of the tunnel or the silver lining. All I saw was darkness and losing people that I loved and knew loved me. But first, forgiving yourself means having the freedom to ask God to forgive you and to ask your loved ones to forgive you. Anyone can say they changed, but their actions will align with their words. I had to talk the talk and walk the walk.

With freedom comes peace. Being deserving of both, the same thing applies to you: you are important, valued, loved, amazing, and stronger than you think... *it's time to be HER!*

You must take personal responsibility. You cannot change the circumstances, the seasons, or the wind, but you can change yourself. That is something you have charge of.

—Jim Rohn

Strength and honor are her clothing, and she shall rejoice in times to come. She openeth her mouth with wisdom, and in her tongue is the law of kindness.

—Proverbs 31:25–26 (KJV)

CHAPTER 1
How to Use

Now that you know a little of my backstory, let's start with expressing yours. Starting off, you will write whatever you feel—the good, bad, or ugly. You are crying out on *your* paper. Take fifteen minutes out of your day to write down your emotions, to release, to exhale, and to get in touch with *you* again.

So, let's get started, shall we? This will be a daily journal, twenty-one days of you pouring yourself out on paper, expressing yourself, telling your secrets to yourself, and embracing who you are. No matter how successful someone may be, everyone experiences insecurities in their lives; this is normal. What is not normal is when you dwell on the insecurities and allow them to control your mood, to control your day, and to change who you are to please your partner, friends, family, or colleagues, etc. These things are not healthy.

Allow God to teach you how to navigate through your insecurities. Your overall value is not what you have obtained—degrees, licenses, certificates, houses, cars, or even looks. It doesn't matter how much you have achieved if you don't believe those things bring value; you'll end up staying in the mindset of feeling like you are not enough.

If you are experiencing any insecurities with your thoughts, what truths are you allowing to take up space within your mind? Your value is not wrapped up in your appearance or your past. Those things don't determine your value or your worth. You and God determine that. Move forward. Your worth is not up for debate. It doesn't matter what actions you have done or what circumstances you have gone through. Remember, everyone has a past. Every sinner has a future, and every saint has a past.

If you allow more self-deprecating thoughts to hold your mind imprisoned, you are diminishing your own value and showing others the same. You are peeling that stamp of approval off of yourself and your worth. Stop it! Are you willing to clear out those insecurities that have taken up the space needed for you to grow?

When those times of anxiety arise, you will then learn how to channel those feelings into calm and pleasant thoughts. At the end of this journal, you can go back and revisit your writings, see how far you have come, and be proud of yourself. Rome was not built in a day, so don't expect to change overnight. This will take practice and consistency.

Our anxiety does not come from thinking about the future, but from wanting to control it.

—Kahlil Gibran

Current Thoughts

Crying out on *your* paper!

The secret of change is to focus all your energy not on fighting the old but on building the new.

—Socrates

CHAPTER 2
Pros and Cons

Before entering a romantic relationship, be sure you are dateable. Wow—harsh, right? No, on the contrary. Dating yourself will improve your relationships of all kinds. Dating yourself helps boost your confidence, and you will get to know yourself better—all of you, not just the facade most people put on to convince others to like them (putting your best foot forward or showing your representative), because we all want to be liked or loved. Have you ever encountered someone who says, "I want people to hate me?" Of course not. But they truly see themselves, down to the innermost, darkest places we sometimes don't know exist or those skeletons we refuse to share with a single soul...

First, let's start with what you feel are your pros and cons. Jot down a few things on both, then go back and really observe those words. Like most of the population, you may find yourself filling up the cons enormously fast and struggling with the pros, but trust me, you have pros. You may need to dig deep and pull them out, but they are there.

Pros	**Cons**

This will help you see if your overacting outbursts were childhood trauma, acceptance issues, struggling with your outer beauty, etc. These could be caused by bullying, neglect, psychological or physical abuse, and tragic life accidents, to list a few.

Loneliness is an opportunity to find yourself. In solitude, you are least alone.

—Bruce Lee

But Jesus often withdrew to lonely places and prayed.

—Luke 5:16

Cons

Now you have written down a few of your pros and cons, starting with your pros. See, I told you that you could do it. After reading your pros, I am sure that they put a smile on your face. Keep those positive notes near your place of view as a reminder to yourself. Sometimes we tend to think about pros and cons as facts and opinions. Pros are facts or truths, and cons are opinions of ourselves.

Let's say you are up for your yearly evaluation at your place of employment. You think you do well just like everyone else, but when you read your review, they see a lot more in you than you ever noticed. How you view yourself is usually not how others view you.

Now, looking at the cons, ask yourself why. This is not a rhetorical question; really ask yourself why this is a con for you. Then answer the question: Is this a fact or your opinion of you?

Con #1

Why do you feel this way?

Explain:

Now answer the question. Is this a fact or is this your opinion of yourself?

FACT ☐ **OPINION** ☐

What can be done to change the outcome?

Con #2

Why do you feel this way?

Explain:

FACT ☐ **OPINION** ☐

What can be done to change the outcome?

Con #3

Why do you feel this way?

Explain:

FACT ☐ **OPINION** ☐

What can be done to change the outcome?

Con #4

Why do you feel this way?

Explain:

FACT ☐ **OPINION** ☐

What can be done to change the outcome?

Con #5

Why do you feel this way?

Explain:

FACT ☐ **OPINION** ☐

What can be done to change the outcome?

Con #6

Why do you feel this way?

Explain:

FACT ☐ **OPINION** ☐

What can be done to change the outcome?

If it turns out to be a fact, can your con be changed? If yes, make a short-term goal to achieve that change. If it comes out to be something you cannot change, such as your nationality or your age, for example, search out self-healing techniques to accept the things that cannot be changed. You can see a professional to help sort through the things that cannot be changed, but accepting who you are is a huge step toward self-awareness and happiness. Everything in life is a choice—the choice to forgive, to trust, to accept, or to love, etc.

It took me a long time not to judge myself through someone else's eyes.

—Sally Field

Short-Term Goals

I know what I want. I have a goal, an opinion. I have a religion and love. Let me be myself, and then I am satisfied. I know that I'm a woman, a woman with inward strength and plenty of courage.

—Anne Frank

CHAPTER 3

Dating Yourself

I want you to think about your last relationship or date that went south *fast*. Write down the incident, and if at the time you received their version of it, write that down as well. Be as detailed as possible. Go back and read it for understanding. Sometimes, when we write things down and go back and read them, we tend to see them in a different light. I have done this. It seems one way or makes sense in my head, but when I write it down, see it physically, and read it, it really isn't what I thought.

Can you pick apart the "errors" and the "mistakes"? Ask yourself, "Why?" Why did I act this way? Why did I get anxiety? What were my triggers?

Incident

Encourage one another and build each other up, just as in fact you are doing.

—Thessalonians 5:11

Reread and see if that "truth" still applies to the incident. If not, ask yourself questions that put your fears about the situation in perspective instead of escalating them. Many times, people will make up scenarios in their heads that may be distorted from the truth. For example, if you get mad at someone and keep replaying the argument in your head, seeing this person afterward might change your view of them. This is unhealthy as your thoughts and memories are a powerful place. When you reflect on the pain you relive that pain all over again, opening that wound over and over allowing your safe, healthy thoughts to be infected. This is the power of our thoughts and memories, and it can lock a person in self-torture, instead of getting their full healing.

When this takes place, you need to make the decision to stop choosing to battle with your thoughts. By doing this, you've turned your mind into a combat zone, waging war against yourself. If not channeled, this will worsen, and the battle will never end. Take a step back from your thoughts. It is important to note the dissimilarity between your thoughts and you. The scene will not change; it will look much the same, but you're not going to continue battling in your mind anymore. Your thoughts will continue to generate, but you're not going to challenge them or investigate them moving forward.

If you're wondering how I know this, it's because I too was stuck in my head for many years. I dealt with unwanted thoughts and fears, and whenever I was supposed to be having a good time or relaxing, I was indeed investigating and cultivating my negative feelings. I could never be present; I feared being alone, and I thought it would never end. This journal is here to help you break free from this torment. Journaling is a way to manage stress and anxious thoughts. The story you tell yourself will be the story that you live. Just remember *you are not your thoughts*!

Getting out of your head helps you experience greater happiness in your everyday life. Aren't you worth it? Your self-talk will work for you or against you. This will leave you in a "not enough" space of shame, or worthlessness, that gets in the way of your self-belonging. On your part, what do you think were your triggers to the downfall of that or that relationship?

We are addicted to our thoughts. We cannot change anything if we cannot change our thinking.

—Santosh Kalwar

CHAPTER 4

Triggers

After carefully reviewing your incident list, what do you think were your triggers—rejection, criticism, anger, emotional detachment, insecurities, fear, lack of boundaries, overthinking, etc.?

Triggers

______________________ ______________________

______________________ ______________________

______________________ ______________________

______________________ ______________________

So, for example, if you find yourself excessively calling someone you care about or love because they said they were going to call you back and now an hour has passed, or they left their house outside of their normal routine, or you're even stalking their social media to try to "put a puzzle together," this is overthinking and a part of the anxious attachment style. These people tend to go straight to the negative. They think it is all about them, not in a conceited kind of way but a negative one, always wondering if someone is mad at them or talking about them, wondering if they did something wrong or even being a "yes man." You can't tell people no for fear of them not liking you. This is the ultimate fear of being abandoned. The majority of the time, everyone is in their own world with their own issues, plans, and goals; they are not worried about you.

In some serious situations like the one listed above, I would suggest seeking out a professional of your choosing—someone who is neutral to your situation—which could be a pastor or even a psychologist to help work through your thoughts and emotions to get to the root of the problem. By doing this, you will be able to start your healing.

Consider this scenario with a tree: Imagine the owner encountering problems with its placement, prompting them to cut it down to the stump. Initially, the issue seems fixed, but without addressing the root cause, the tree inevitably regrows. Therefore, faced with a choice: repeatedly patch up the wound, like applying Band-Aids to a deep cut, or delve deep to unearth the underlying issue. It may be arduous, perhaps painful, but by persisting and addressing the root cause, you liberate your mind from its constraints, achieving true freedom.

Story Time: In my early twenties, I was told once, "If you look for dirt, you'll find it." My bright response was, "If there was no dirt, I wouldn't find it." Hmm, no... It took some time to understand what that statement really meant. Our minds like to fill in the blanks (apophenia) that are missing in the puzzle; if we have a negative mindset, our thoughts will go straight to the bad. As you dig, so to speak, the thing(s) that you find may not be true or a fact, for things aren't always what they seem.

What you see is not what others see. We inhabit parallel worlds of perception, bounded by our interests and experience. What is obvious to some is invisible to others.

—George Monbiot

With perception, the first thing is the selection stage. This is where we allow that selection to attend to our senses. Then it will process through the organization stage. This is where we want to sort this information. Finally, the last stage is interpretation, and this is where we attach the meaning. Since we are humans and we attach our meaning to it, there is a possibility that your perception of it may not be what you thought. This could be a result of that person's previous action or your experiences with that certain situation. But I will say this: even if their previous actions were so, ask yourself, "Do I see change?" Are they conducting themselves as they did previously? If not, give them the benefit of the doubt; allow facts to prove them differently.

Story Time: While my husband and I were on the road driving, I was looking out the window into the far distance. I then noticed some young women in the car beside us, staring at me with a "What are you looking at?" stare.

Perplexed, I told my husband, and his response was unexpected: "You were looking at them." Honestly, I wasn't. I hadn't noticed them until that moment. It was a stark reminder that sometimes people's perceptions can differ from reality—it's not always about you.

I was always taught growing up that there are three sides to every story: his, hers, and the truth. That is not to say that anyone is lying; that is just the version of *their* truth. Also, have you ever heard the phrase, "Believe nothing you hear and only half of what you see"? At times, our eyes can be deceived. There was an image illustrating the concept of perception: a lioness holding her cub in her mouth. From one angle, it appeared as though the cub was injured or lifeless, with its head seemingly inside the lioness's mouth. However, upon shifting to the other side, it became evident that the cub was unharmed; the lioness was simply carrying her offspring. This is the same thing with hearing.

Story Time: I remember in high school when one of my teachers did an experiment. He whispered instructions to the first person in the row and then told that person to repeat them verbatim to the person behind them and keep going to the last person in class. Needless to say, by the time it reached the last person in class, it wasn't remotely the same as the original statement. So try to take things with a grain of salt and gather the facts before jumping to any conclusions.

Side Note: In addition, a wise woman once told me, "Watch the dog that carries the bone." Everyone has a motive. Now, I am not saying everyone's motive is malicious and deceiving; some may be, yes, but that's not the case for the majority. But remember, there is always a motive.

CHAPTER 5
Continue Dating Yourself

Dating yourself comes with putting yourself first, but this is *selfish*! "I am not a selfish person," you say; this is far from the truth. Putting yourself first is healthy. While dating yourself builds self-confidence and self-esteem. When you get on a plane and the flight attendant gives their instructions for the oxygen masks, they tell you to put the mask on first before you try to help anyone else. The same is true with your health. What is the purpose of chasing money, working yourself to the bone, if your health is at risk? You aren't eating and drinking correctly. This short-lived abundance of money would all be in vain; you would no longer be here, and where would your money go? Not with you, so would it be worth it?

When I was born into this world, I was naked and had nothing. When I die and leave this world, I will be naked and have nothing.

—Job 1:21 (ERV)

Same thing with you: you are running around trying to please everyone else, doing things for everyone as they benefit, and you fill up with stress while depleting yourself of peace. At the end of the day, what have you done for yourself? Did you take some time out to breathe and recoup? I guarantee you, your answer will be no. We must change this. Putting you first is not selfish; putting you first is setting boundaries and is necessary. Putting your physical and mental health first is not selfish. Taking time out for you, doing what you love, is not being selfish. You must charge yourself back up.

I heard a story one time: "Two lumberjacks challenged each other to see how many trees they could cut down in a single day. One lumberjack started right off while the other spent forty-five minutes sharpening his saw. The first lumberjack mocked the second, felling tree after tree. But as time went on, the first lumberjack fell to fatigue from the extra work of using a dull blade, quitting early in the afternoon. The second lumberjack continued his work until the evening and claimed the victory. His sharpened saw had enhanced his natural capabilities."

What I got out of this story is that you must take time out, and in this case, take time out for yourself—time to rest and enjoy yourself by yourself, just to be free. By doing this, your senses will be enhanced. Have you ever done a word search and an hour or so passes, and you just can't find that last word? You put it down and walk away, change your scenery, rest your eyes, then come back, and within a minute, you find the word. You recharged yourself.

Putting yourself first is the first step to real love. You will have to love yourself first before anyone else can love you. If you can't stand to be out on a date with you, how do you expect anyone else to? When you love yourself first, you are teaching others how to treat you. Being insecure and not knowing your true power, you will accept things you know are not right, but with the fear of losing that person, you feel it is greater than how they treat you.

Dating yourself and putting yourself first will help you build self-reliance and practice independence. By enjoying your own company, you will then be comfortable and can see clearer when you allow someone to enter your space.

Story Time: I was married at a young age. I did everything with my husband or with at least one friend. When he passed, my four children were all under the age of twelve. I didn't know how to do things by *myself*. But I told myself, "You can do this." It was awkward at first, but I took myself out. If I wanted to see a movie, I would go by myself and watch an evening movie, at that. Sometimes I would get dressed up and go to a sit-down restaurant. It took some time to really feel comfortable with myself to do this, but now, I prefer it.

Now, let's write a few ideas down; what are some takeaways, thoughts, or ideas you are having? You don't have to rush out and start tomorrow, but you can say, "Next Saturday, I am going to treat myself to..." Try something outside your norm. People can go to the mall by themselves or get their manicure or pedicure by themselves; think outside the box. Maybe start small—take a nature trail walk, start with a daytime movie, and work your way up to that nighttime movie (We all know everyone goes out on their dates to those nighttime movies. LOL), go make a reservation at a restaurant, go to new dance classes, go to a sip and paint...the ideas are endless when it comes to self-love.

Notes, Ideas, Thoughts

Happiness is when what you think, what you say, and what you do are in harmony.

—Mahatma Gandhi

Dating Yourself Ideas

________________________	________________________
________________________	________________________
________________________	________________________
________________________	________________________
________________________	________________________
________________________	________________________

I promise you, if you continue to date and treat yourself, you will start to like your own company, and you'll start really falling in love with *you*! Do for you what you want your future spouse or others to do. I buy myself flowers all the time. I expect him to open the door, pull out my chair, walk on the outer side of the sidewalk, etc. I am very romantic; chivalry is not dead with me. I don't care about your past mistakes. We all have them. No one is perfect, intended or not. Your past is now in stone; that cannot change. Forgive yourself and focus on your now. Today is your present, and tomorrow is a blessing. Why? Because you are deserving of it.

* * *

Now, you took yourself on your date. Yay! I am so proud of you. Write down your feelings, thoughts, and experiences in detail below. Detail is key here.

By doing the work to love ourselves more, I believe we will love each other better.

—Sally Field

First Date Experience

____

____

____

____

____

Owning our story and loving ourselves through that process is the bravest thing that we'll ever do.

—Brené Brown

Go back and revisit what you wrote. Is there anything you would change? As the time went by, did you start to feel more at ease and more comfortable? Jot down a few ideas for your next outing or doing the same thing, but maybe this time in the evening. Yes, you will have three more dates with yourself within your twenty-one-day journaling process.

As you start to have more interactions like this with yourself, your confidence will grow tremendously. People told me I was weird or crazy for going out by myself, or others would say, "Oh, I could never do that." Trust me—yes, you can. Just take that first step.

Story Time: I made reservations at Abuelo's, which is a nice local restaurant with chandeliers, a pianist, dim lighting, a very romantic atmosphere, etc. All these couples were to my left, to my right, in front of me, and behind me, and I was literally sitting in the center of the room by myself. I was wearing a black dress with heels and a black brim hat, which is sexy and classy if you ask me. LOL. I felt the stares, and if we made eye contact, I just gave a smile and a head nod. Just because it is not everyone's norm doesn't make it erroneous.

By taking yourself out, you are enjoying your life. Do what brings you joy and happiness, and that'll put a genuine smile on your face. You deserve it. Read a book, make a vision board, listen to music in your living room, and dance like no one is watching. Pick up a new hobby, something you may have been putting off for a while. Your mind is your only limitation.

You have to date yourself first; I cannot express that enough. You don't want to torture yourself and bring anxiety back into your life that will bombard your mind. When this takes place, it takes you out of reality and into a prison of your mind; you are physically there, but your mind is ten thousand miles away. You can forget things and put important projects or tasks aside because you are dwelling on—get this—the "what if" factor and not the facts.

I cannot give credit to the person since I don't remember the name, but I heard if you are an overthinker, ask yourself this question: "Where is the fact?" This is so true; you are trying to put the puzzle together without having all the pieces, and by doing so, you are creating your own puzzle outcome with *your nonfactual perception*, and most likely, those "fill in the blank" pieces are filled with negative thoughts. Stop it! When this occurs, take a moment, step back, and question it; if you need to write down the *facts* of the situation and see what you come up with, then do it.

You don't have to be in control of everything. You can't, as a matter of fact. You can only control you—your thoughts, your emotions, and your actions. If you continue to try to control everything, you will eventually push your loved one away. Having self-control is important in everyday living. 2 Timothy 1:7 (ERV) says, "The spirit God gave us does not make us afraid. His spirit is a source of power and love and self-control." If you start to get anxious, break your mind away, read a book, change your environment, and start to channel those thoughts and feelings in your journal. Then, go back and read your facts. No one wants to live in torture, and worst of all, self-torture.

Notes, Ideas, Thoughts

She is more precious than rubies; nothing you desire can compare with her. Long life is in her right hand; in her left hand are riches and honor. Her ways are pleasant ways, and all her paths are peace. She is a tree of life to those who take hold of her; those who hold her fast will be blessed.

—Proverbs 3:15–18

To love oneself is the beginning of a lifelong romance.

—Oscar Wilde

CHAPTER 6

Be Soft

I am asking you to be soft. This is not jumping on the "soft" trend of influencers, but really becoming soft. As we witness this world becoming hard, don't allow it to make you hard; we cannot afford dilution of what we believe. Refuse to live in the grayness of this world but arrive to a situation with perspective and prevail. Life is sensitive, sometimes fragile, but it is also flexible. Life can be soft if we allow it to be.

So run to that place, whatever that shall be, that brings an honest smile to your face. Your mental well-being for a happy life is not just about personal self-actualization but also the love of those around you and that you are sincerely happy within yourself. Do not allow others to have control over how your day would be. You would be giving them power over you. Take your power back.

Embrace self-love and prioritize it, recognizing that perfection is an illusion. Allow God to fill you with love completely while mending the broken pieces of your heart in His presence. Trust in Him, letting go of doubts, letting God wipe away your tears and provide solace when most needed.

While it is impossible to rewrite the past, you can start now and craft a brand-new ending. Yet today marks the new beginning of an exciting chapter ahead, one that requires patience, time, understanding, consistency, and faith. Stay modest, stay grounded, and stay self-assured through your journey of journaling and new adventures; this will bring that fresh conclusion. You are worthy and enough. Being enough means recognizing that you don't need to change or add anything beyond your authentic self to receive love and acceptance It's the unconditional love that you will have for yourself that is encountered with compassion and understanding, regardless of your flaws or shortcomings.

For you to believe that you're enough, recognize that your great qualities offset the not-so-great ones. If you are struggling with self-doubt, it becomes easy to fall into that deception of believing you are not good enough. But the truth is that you are. Become that person who is irreplaceable!

Life can be painful; sometimes it's the process of the pain that's significant and essential to help you put things in perspective when you didn't see them before. I believe every pain is dissimilar; some sting more than others. Pain is as different as someone's fingerprints. So, I encourage you to go through that pain and allow it to make you stronger, wiser, and even more powerful, but most of all, allow it to heal the broken pieces that you tell no one about. Just because you don't see it now doesn't mean it won't be in your season to come. Stay encouraged, stay patient, and stay focused. In this time, build. Build the best you. Would you want someone to receive a good version of you, or the best version?

Don't allow the pain of the past to make you hate; don't allow bitterness to steal your sweetness; don't forget who and whose you are. You are worth loving. Stay focused, continue to move with the flow of time, and embrace patience with a soft touch, for God is the healer of all pain; allow Him to soften your heart.

Forgiveness is not an occasional act. It is a permanent attitude.

—Dr. Martin Luther King Jr.

There are levels to everything, so keep pushing through each one of them to get to your journey's end. There is a natural softness about us; we must become water. Water can be calm, powerful, strong, forgiving, adaptable, and fierce in its respective time and place.

My interpretation of men and women would be, "Men are truth; women are grace." Truth comes before grace. The saying is "truth hurts," right? So, men are truth; if his son did something wrong and needs to be disciplined, that man, husband, father will come with truth. He will possibly whoop him then sit him down and explain to his son the reasoning behind his punishment; truth hurts. Then comes women—the grace. Grace is forgiving, soft, calm, and uplifting, so when a woman, wife, mother comes, she comes to rebuild her son and give love and encouragement. Now, this does not mean she will go against the father; hear me correctly. Discipline should be on the same page, but men and women have different roles in the discipline process.

Men are attracted to soft, feminine women. Masculinity will match with femininity always. Have you ever seen a masculine woman? She will have a feminine man, and vice versa. Be soft; be nice to strangers. A man is watching how you move, what you say, your body language, and the twitch of your nose. He is learning you. We are love; we are natural nurturers, so become that. It is OK and encouraged to have a guard up at first. Allow a gate around your heart, not an unbreakable brick wall. No, you don't want to spill your whole life story onto someone new—and to be honest, that would be a red flag.

Stay mysterious, show yourself love and appreciation, go out with your girlfriends, go out with yourself, and don't be afraid to date you first. Have goals, create habits, and produce outcomes.

Story Time: No marriage or relationship is perfect. I think we all can agree on this. But two people putting God first and trying is worth it. Toward the last days of my husband being here on earth, my husband showed power, knowing oneself, and knowing his place in God. As stated previously, my late husband, Quintero A. Scott Sr., was diagnosed with a chronic liver disease at the young age of seventeen years old. I knew this when we got married. His father, Donald L. Wesley, received a liver transplant and lived many years later. So we thought yes, we will have to go through the hardship of the transplant and hospital visits, but he will get a transplant and live happily ever after, right? Unfortunately, this is not how my story unfolded.

Toward the end, he was lethargic and was admitted to Tampa General Hospital (TGH) ICU. I lived at TGH for months. His liver had totally failed him, and even with dialysis three times a week, his kidneys were failing fast. He had five liver offers, but something was wrong with every one of them. I remember the doctors coming in and asking me all types of questions that I didn't understand. I said, "This has nothing to do with his liver." They eventually told me they found cancer—a type of cancer that was untouchable. With a transplant, your immune system is extremely weakened to accept the foreign organ, even though it is there to help. He was too sick to go back on the transplant list.

He had so many doctors: liver, kidney, blood, bone, and so on. They all loved him and were fighting for him. A lady came and asked to speak with me in private. We went to a conference room, and she said she had to talk to me about something.

I said, "The only thing you could tell me is that he is no longer eligible to go back on the list." I said, "Please wait, and let me call his mother." I had his mom on speaker phone, and the lady began to explain the doctor's findings.

She asked, "How do you think Mr. Scott will respond to this news?"

I said, "He will be hurt, but he will say thank you."

With a shocked look on her face, she said, "Thank you?"

I said, "Yes, he will say thank you."

We walked back to his room; he had just returned from a dialysis treatment, and he was sitting in the recliner chair. All the other doctors who were treating him for something of every kind were waiting for her and me to reach his closed room door. As his door opened, he looked at all his doctors and specialists in the hallway, and he began to cry; he knew.

As everyone entered his room, I sat on his bed beside him, handing him some tissues. One doctor explained the findings. He then asked him, "Mr. Scott, do you understand? Do you have any questions?"

He looked around at everyone and said, "I know you all did everything that you could do, and I want to thank you. God knows my time."

They were all shocked by his response and him taking it so well. But he knew who he was in God.

About a week had passed, and now he was in step-down ICU, still doing dialysis three times a week. A young doctor came in, and he asked to go home.

The doctor said, "Mr. Scott, the extent of your life is here."

He said, "I know. I just want to go home. I want to see my kids."

Her response was, "Mr. Scott, if you go home, you will decline and decline fast."

He said, "I know. I still want to go home. I want to be with my family. It is time for me to go if I start to overwhelm Jojo."

Even writing this now brings tears to my eyes. What kind of love is this? He was willing to die to not overwhelm me. I said, "Tiger, no. It is your time to go when God says it is your time to go, not me."

Before they would agree to let him come home, I had to set up his dialysis schedule. Tiger was discharged on a Thursday; he had his dialysis on Friday, where he slept for the remainder of the day, which was normal. He was lethargic on Saturday.

I sat beside him on the bed. I was holding his hand, and he started to shake his head back and forth as if fighting it. I held his hand tighter and said, "Tiger, it's OK, it's OK. We are here." He calmed some, and with his eyes closed the whole time, I said, "Tiger, I love you; do you love me?"

He then opened his eyes, searched for me, nodded his head yes, then took three breaths and ended up passing at 2:00 a.m. on Sunday morning.

Out of that story, I really wanted you to get one thing that he said: "It is time for me to go if I start to overwhelm Jojo." His words hit me like a ton of bricks. He would rather die than stress me out, really. This is love. God said in Ephesians 5:25, "Husbands, love your wives, just as Christ loved the church and gave himself up for her." That is exactly what he was willing to do.

If you want to get married one day, listen to the vows that you will take. Ask yourself one question: Are you willing to lay your life down for that person?

Side Note: One thing in my marriage that I learned was "You do what you got to do to keep peace in your home." This does not mean you will become a doormat. Sometimes it is best to "give up the right to be right," meaning, is it really worth the fight or the battle? More times than not, your answer would be no.

Let's say there is a small get-together with some close friends of yours and your man brings up something that was originally your idea. Now, how will you react? Are you a woman who'll say, "Now, bae, you know that was my idea." Or are you a woman who will say, "Bae, that's a great idea." Now, bae knows it was your idea. LOL. But does everyone need to know it was originally yours? No.

If you choose to act out and demand to get credit for your idea, this will bring embarrassment, humiliation and bruise this man's ego. All of this would make him feel less of a man, and more likely than not, this will end with an argument and hopefully not a disagreement in front of your friends.

What just happened was this: You may have won the fight (letting everyone know it was your idea), but you lost the battle (your husband's ego and pride are now bruised by your hand). What's going to happen is that your drive home will be in silence, or there will be an argument. When you guys get home, there is going to be silent treatment, more arguing, going to bed mad, etc.

Was being "right" worth it? I hope your answer is no. This doesn't mean you can't express yourself; you can, but just at the right time. One of the worst things a woman or a wife can do is make her husband feel less of a man, especially in front of people. Let's normalize uplifting, encouraging, and respecting his position as a man, husband, and leader. You chose to marry this man; you chose his leadership over your life, so accept it. This will only benefit you in the long run. Treat him as you want him to treat you; would you have wanted him to do that to you if the roles were reversed?

Make him feel needed; this is important. Let's say you are opening a new jar of pickles. Yes, your amazing self can open a jar of pickles, but I would recommend walking up to him and asking him to open it for you. Then, look at him and say, "I don't know what I'd do without you." I'm telling you, once you say that, watch his demeanor change. See him smiling, watch his chest puff out... Being this type of woman, asking him to be your "Superman", he would find it difficult to leave this type of woman who empowers him to embody the man he aspires to be. He seeks to perceive his greatness reflected in your eyes, finding validation and fulfillment in feeling needed and esteemed. In your presence, you epitomize the essence of femininity by affirming his sense of worth and importance.

Another subject that every man thinks he has going on is in the bedroom. If he does something you are not quite fond of, don't tear this man down, telling him he's "not doing it right." On the other hand, don't keep it to yourself; you want to be pleasured too. If he really loves and cares for you, he will listen. He'll listen to how you moan or move, etc. So, when he does something you don't like, don't make any noise or guide him where you want him to be. Teach him how to love you. It's the same for what you really enjoy; let him know this. A few days later, when he's in the kitchen making a sandwich, walk up behind him, put your arms around him, and whisper in his ear, "I really enjoyed it when you did XYZ. I'm looking forward to that again." And just simply walk away and do whatever you were going to do. He'll take a mental note.

A perfect marriage is just two imperfect people who refuse to give up on each other.

—Unknown

With this, if you are not married and would like to become a wife, list some important qualities that you are looking for in your future husband; even if you are not talking to anyone, write these down.

Qualities in Your Future Husband

______________________	______________________
______________________	______________________
______________________	______________________
______________________	______________________
______________________	______________________
______________________	______________________

The key is to be as specific as possible. Ask what you need, what you want, and what you deserve. Now, can one person be all these things? Maybe that could be tough, but if he is not all these things and is missing two or three, what are they? Are these dealbreakers? If not, then weigh it out.

Story Time: A lot of people believe common sense is the same for everyone, but in fact, it is not; common sense comes from someone's upbringing, experiences, environment, etc. This develops their common sense. Not everyone's common sense is the same. I think it is common sense that when you walk in a room, you acknowledge the people in the room, even if it is just a head nod, but some people don't think like this. Now, does this make them wrong and me right? No; that is my perception on common sense. I said that to say this: As you know by now, I was with my husband at a young age, and with no life experiences, I became a widow. I was living my twenties—the "error" stage, the "oops" stage, or the "wow, I didn't expect that to happen" stage, and so on. A lot of people would say, "But you are not in your twenties; this is common sense." Well, in fact, no, this was not my common sense; I never lived it. I didn't have experience in this part of life.

When my husband finds me, he will get the best version of me. With my life experiences and getting older, I learned. Being married and experiencing things within the marriage, I learned. With the passing of my husband and having regrets, I learned. Now, being a single mother, I learned. Having numerous failed dating experiences, I learned. With these experiences, I would say I know the importance of not taking someone for granted.

Below, there is space to write down your prayer for your husband. Pray over his mind, heart, spirit, relationship with God, you, your kids, and so on. Speak it as so.

Everything means nothing if I ain't got you.

—Alicia Keys

Future Husband Prayer

I can't fall in love without you.

—Zara Larsson

Also, be genuine; just remember, no one is perfect, and he also has his list of what he is looking for in a woman. The bible states in Proverbs 18:22 (KJV) that "Whoso findeth a wife findeth a good thing, and obtaineth favour of the Lord." Now, you may ask the question, "How can I be a wife before becoming a wife?" Good question. Being a wife before officially becoming one involves embodying the qualities and characteristics that contribute to a strong and fulfilling marital relationship. Being a wife before marriage is about preparing yourself mentally, emotionally, spiritually, and practically for the responsibilities and blessings of marriage. It's about embodying the qualities of a loving and supportive partner and nurturing a mindset of commitment, sacrifice, and partnership. A wife is the crown of her husband; she is loyal and the perfect helper. God doesn't tell women to love their husbands because we are love. That is in our DNA. But He calls us to respect our husbands. Be his safe haven and his safe place to rest. Women tend to treat men as we want to be treated. Men view love differently; love and respect are one and the same to him, as love and security are one and the same to women. Be the person you want to attract.

Become that wife that you want your husband to become. If you desire him to be loyal, you will be loyal; if you desire him to dress classy, you will dress classy, etc. Lyfe Jennings made a song called "Statistic." Be that woman. Tell him that you are celibate. Hold yourself pure until you are married. What better way to honor your husband than to hold yourself for him? If a man is not willing to stay with you, wanting to live with boundaries, morals, and respect for yourself, then he is just not the one for you. Lyfe Jennings also stated, "Be the person that you want to find; don't be a nickel out here, lookin' for a dime." Be on an equal level. Match, so to speak. Keep up your appearance and show respect with the choice of clothes you wear. Yes, a lot of guys will approach you if you are showing yourself off, but those are boys and not men. Those guys won't have a problem taking you home and showing you a good time, but when it is all said and done, you will be on to the next.

What if you are already married? Prayer still works. Pray for what you need him to be, and if you are asking him to be that, you will become the same as his wife. If you want him to be more loving and caring, you should be that to him; if you desire more compliments, give them to him. At the end of the day, make sure you have done all that you could to make it work. Maybe look at yourself. How can you become a better wife? Take some time and list a few things that you know you could work on.

Working on My "Wife"

______________________	______________________
______________________	______________________
______________________	______________________
______________________	______________________
______________________	______________________
______________________	______________________

There is no perfect person, and we are all different in our ways. Let love seep in by becoming a better *her*.

CHAPTER 7

What's New

When developing a habit, there is a 21/90 rule: it takes twenty-one days to create a habit and ninety days to make it a permanent lifestyle change. While you start journaling daily, you'll find it will become easier as time progresses, becoming second nature. Plus, you can dedicate as much or as little time as you feel you need. I would recommend a minimum of fifteen minutes a day.

Remember, journaling is writing in ways to generate more love for yourself, to obtain self-compassion for yourself. As you cultivate greater compassion for yourself, it blossoms into happiness, drawing others toward you as they begin to take notice. Take this time to write any updates, thoughts, feelings, emotions, new dates with yourself, and anything else you may have since you started your journaling process.

What's New?

As I began to love myself, I stopped craving for a different life, and I could see that everything that surrounded me was inviting me to grow.

—Charlie Chaplin

Below, take some small notes on your "What's New?" journaling. Were your feelings managed, controlled, and rationally thought through?

Don't justify your feelings during this process. If you're sad, write about how it feels to be sad. No explanations are needed. This is for you to help see yourself and grow.

☐ Identify your feelings:

____

____

____

After writing down your feelings, was there anything that caused this trigger?

☐ Were there triggers?:

____

____

____

Ask yourself: Was this a positive or negative encounter? Why did I react this way?

☐ Your emotions:

____

____

____

Does your journaling expose something about you and how you handle this emotion?

☐ Reflect:

____

____

____

- [ ] Have you seen change in your reaction?:

___

___

___

Once you start to embrace your newfound self-love, your eyes will be opened to so many things. Your confidence will increase; you will set aside and dedicate time to just you, knowing that you are important and won't accept anything less. If you don't allow yourself to fall in love with you, all of you, you will have this sense of continuously searching for something that you will never reach or fulfill, having that feeling of emptiness.

Self-love, my liege, is not so vile a sin as self-neglecting.

—William Shakespeare

CHAPTER 8

Let's Talk

If you continuously tell those around you negative things, expressing your flaws, people will start to focus on that flaw, most likely a flaw that you created. Eventually, they will start to believe you. If you tell someone something long enough, they will believe it. In addition, stop asking people for their opinion. It is OK to ask someone for their opinion; I mean not excessively, where you cannot make the decision on your own. Learn to develop the muscle of your own opinion; self-worth also comes when you can rely on your own judgment.

An example would be...well, let me just tell you my story. In middle school, I was picked on. Kids would tease me all the time about my eyes; they would say they were big and even call me Kermit the Frog. How cruel, right? I know. LOL. I would grow my bangs out to literally cover my eyes. Yes, that long. Silly, I know. But by being told all the time that my eyes were big, I started to believe them. I started to see that my eyes were a problem that stuck with me even into adulthood. I would still try to hide them. I would still tell people how I didn't like my eyes until recently.

But now, I embrace my eyes. Do you know what? The first thing people compliment me on is...you guessed it—*my eyes*! By changing the way I saw the situation and choosing not to focus on what I thought looked bad, that became the number one compliment that I receive. So, the "flaw" that I saw really wasn't a flaw at all.

Continue dating yourself. Let's talk to yourself.

The more you spend time alone with yourself, the more you find your strengths and weaknesses. You'll draw closer to yourself and God. You will appreciate you loving and taking care of you. By doing this, you are teaching yourself how you will allow others to treat you. You won't allow people to come in and disturb your peace. You will be so in tune with you that you won't jeopardize anyone coming in and destroying what you worked so hard for—*you*.

You can start your verbal affirmation with a compliment. I've heard people talk down to themselves. I have caught myself doing it from time to time. The power of life or death is in our tongue. Ever heard the phrase, "You are what you speak"? Do you ever say or hear someone say, "Man, I'm so stupid," or, "I can never get this right," after they make a mistake? Your brain does not know the difference, so stop it!

You should speak life into you. When I wake up, the first thing I do is thank God for allowing my family and I to see another day, for protection over us, for being vigilant for what the day may bring, and so on. After that, I talk to myself. That's right...I talk to myself. In my bedroom, I have eight-foot closet mirror doors, and on the top, they say, "You are Enough." And in my bathroom, I have a mirror frame that states, "You are Beautiful." Sometimes, you just must remind yourself who you are.

"Good Morning Gorgeous" by Mary J. Blige is a song that embraces self-confidence, self-love, motivation, and empowerment. Overall, "Good Morning Gorgeous" celebrates femininity, strength, and beauty. It's a reminder for you to embrace yourself fully and to start each day with confidence and grace. I would suggest listening to this song. I find it to be uplifting, boosts my mood and reminds me of my inner strength and beauty.

Compliments and affirmations are wonderful tools to help deter your mind from adverse thinking to positive thoughts. I have even taken "I want" off my statements and replaced it with "I am," "I will," etc. I won't get stuck in the "want." Want means you don't have it, and there is a possibility you won't. But if you say "am," you are creating that positive atmosphere to make it happen and to trust and believe that God will make it happen with your works.

Compliment yourself when you get up in the morning. Before you take a shower, brush your hair, or put on your makeup, look at your pure, raw self, and tell yourself you are beautiful. If you can, do it naked in the mirror—and yes, I'm serious. Tell yourself you are beautiful, compassionate, or whatever you want it to be. After you get all dolled up, go back to the mirror and tell yourself you are an amazing, beautiful, strong, and powerful woman, and you will have an amazing day regardless of what it brings. We trick the brain to act, do, and think about what we say. Research has shown that speaking positive self-talk daily will improve self-esteem, stress management, and your well-being. Also, this can reduce symptoms of anxiety and depression. That's the power of talking to ourselves. By making this a priority, we can strengthen our self-esteem.

Dress up more; when you dress up, you feel alive, confident, important, and empowered. Remember the last time you dressed up for a wedding, an event, or a party? Didn't you walk with confidence, hold your head up, and even smile more? I'm sure you did. So, dress up often, even if it is going to your local grocery store. LOL. Seriously, people don't know where you are going or coming from.

Dressing up will become a habit, and along with that, confidence will increase, and people will notice. Did you know that men are attracted to confident women? Yep, men are natural hunters, and that feeling of you being a challenge just because you are confident in yourself, is attractive. You don't have to be a beauty queen; be confident, own it, and show up like you own that place. Catch that? I said men and not boys.

Story Time: I went to an event, and yes, I was sexy, but I was also fully clothed. I stood outside, leaning against a lofty tabletop, patiently awaiting the completion of the sound check by the next jazz band. Now, in my head, I was talking to myself, reminding myself who I am. I finally walked in, stepped foot in the entrance, and stopped. I glanced at all four corners of the room, gave a small smile, and then walked slowly to where I wanted to stand. While I was halfway in the room, three young women around their mid-twenties stopped me and said, "You are so beautiful; we were watching you outside and couldn't wait for you to come in. You walked into this place like you owned it."

Now, did those young ladies know I was just outside, giving myself a pep talk and hyping myself up like I was about to enter the arena? Nope. What they saw was my confidence! My walk was slow, my head lifted, my shoulders back, my torso long, and a smile on my face...my confidence!

Let's talk a little about the power of your walk, your smile, and a woman's body language. People appear more attractive when they walk with confidence. Like above, I gave myself a pep talk; I knew I had to be confident. So, let's say you want to walk into a room, and you want your presence to be captivating. You will have your head high and your torso tall, and when you walk in, you should walk in with slow strides. Research has shown that people who walk slower are seen as more confident, noticed, and attractive. So, you will walk in with slow strides, get a few steps in, and stop. Look at the four corners of the room. Find someone to look at and smile and then walk to your destination. I guarantee you that you will be noticed. Everyone will be drawn to your charisma, positive appearance, and, yep, confidence.

Side Note: Keep your eyes open to the people who always say what they are to other people—I am this, or I am that. A reason behind this is that they are insecure within themselves and, because of this, overcompensating with words, and they are trying to convince themselves and you that they are what they are saying. Conversational self-focus, or egocentrism, pertains to the tendency of individuals to consistently steer conversations toward themselves. While this behavior may come across as egotistical and insensitive, it often stems from underlying depression. This self-focusing tendency can result in rejection, further exacerbating feelings of depression. However, it is possible to break this cycle. Everyone is different, but usually people with low self-esteem will do this. They are worried about their own opinion of themselves and want to paint this nice image of themselves for others to see. People who are confident make themselves open and tall and tend to refrain from talking excessively about themselves. When you have confidence, you remove that possibility by making it clear in no uncertain terms who you are. For example, does a king walk around his palace, stopping people and telling them, “Hey, I’m the king”? Or does a rich man walk around telling strangers he’s rich? No; they lack the necessity to persuade others as they have a firm understanding of their own identity.

A few facts about smiling are that it does help lower blood pressure, relax you, and boost your immune system. You can trick your brain into thinking you are in a better mood just by simply smiling. It is scientifically proven that people are drawn to people who smile often because they appear more attractive, trustworthy, and positive. So, *smile!* I am more on the serious side, so I have to remind myself to smile most of the time...LOL.

In addition to a woman's body language, you want to be open with your shoulders back—chin up, sit tall, and so on. If you slouch, cross your arms in front of you, or keep your head down, first, you would not be considered approachable by anyone, and second, you would be viewed as insecure. As a side note, this vulnerability might make you susceptible to being manipulated by a man who simply aims to use you. He might offer flattering words that appeal to your desires, finding it effortless to deceive you. Generally, if a man's intention is to toy with a woman, he's less likely to approach someone he perceives as confident. Why would he? It would be too much of a challenge. He might think, "She's got her stuff together; just dropping a compliment won't get me far."

With this, yes, maybe fewer males will approach you, but I would rather have the few that do approach me looking for something real, something that I am looking for as well. Who wants to weed through a bunch of boys? Not me.

Too often, we underestimate the power of a touch, a smile, a kind word, a listening ear, an honest compliment, or the smallest act of caring, all of which have the potential to turn a life around.

—Leo Buscaglia

CHAPTER 9

Loving Yourself

Let's start with giving you what you want from others: compliments. Remember, do to you what you want others to do. Below, let's start by writing down a few compliments about yourself. It can be absolutely anything.

Compliments

______________________ ______________________

______________________ ______________________

______________________ ______________________

______________________ ______________________

By giving yourself daily compliments, you will feel better about yourself, and they will help remind you of your importance and how awesome you are. Allow it to boost your mood, give you a reason to smile, and give you a boost of confidence.

Because it is one thing to have an insecurity or self-doubt, but it's another thing to accept that insecurity to determine your value, and it's yet another thing to look for confirmation from other people that you shouldn't have value.

Compliments cost nothing, yet many pay dear for them.

—Thomas Fuller

Loving Yourself

Now, moving on to affirmations. Affirmations go along the same lines as compliments; our brain processes both of them in a similar way. Write down a few affirmations that you want to tell yourself every day. This is not limited to just when you wake up in the mornings. This is whenever a negative thought tries to enter your mind. When you start feeling down or if something negative just happened to you, you can always start off with a generic affirmation: "I am beautiful," "I am enough," "Today will be a great day," and so on. But let's try to focus on specific affirmations that pertain to you.

Affirmations

______________________	______________________
______________________	______________________
______________________	______________________
______________________	______________________
______________________	______________________
______________________	______________________

When these thoughts come, the key is not to dwell on them. Break that thought. Move, get up from where you are, open a book, listen to a podcast, but do something to break that negative thought.

You can write small love notes to yourself. Place them at your desk at work, on your mirror in your room, or anywhere!

Courage starts with showing up and letting ourselves be seen.

—Brené Brown

CHAPTER 10

What's on Your Mind?

Notes, Ideas, Thoughts

Peace begins with a smile.

—Mother Teresa

CHAPTER 11

You

You want to start doing things for yourself, even if it means getting your nails done every three weeks, but start somewhere. You don't work as hard as you do to not see the fruit of your labor. Don't feel bad about doing something for you. By doing things for you and by yourself, you create benefits doing things for yourself.

1. Sparks creativity.
2. Increases mental strength.
3. Allows you to gain a new perspective.
4. Teaches you to be OK with being alone.
5. Allows you to get to know yourself.
6. Allows you to trust yourself.

When you start doing things by yourself, it takes a degree of confidence and initiative to do things alone and people will notice. Being alone does not mean you are lonely. It means you value yourself and your time, and shoot—you love yourself.

This, I would have to say, is my first time really being alone. When I started back dating, even if I wasn't in a relationship, I always talked to someone, had a conversation of some sort. So, with my earnestness, being alone is giving me new perspectives on my life and what is truly important.

A suggestion I will throw in there is to take a break; take a break from social media. It can be addicting to scroll and watch everyone's lives unfold before you. You never saw little Johnny in person—you never met him—but you see this young boy grow up in life. I mean, am I wrong?

Many times, more often than not, we will fall into a state of depression because we are looking at these "perfect" couples, these "amazing" and "successful" people that we may or may not have encountered in life. But the irony about social media is that you can become anyone you want. They are posting their highlight reels of their lives, where all you see are your bloopers. People post what they want others to see: their best filtered pictures, best videos, best quotes, and perfect relationships. They can become whoever they want to be on social media. This is not 100 percent of their lives. You have those as well: that one favorite picture, that video that captured your full self-happiness, the inspirational quotes that you shared. Don't compare yourself with social media.

No one has it all together 100 percent of the time. You are unique, you are special, you are valued, and you are loved. But you must first see all of that within yourself. If you don't, people will take advantage of that. Everyone has a motive. So, take a break from social media, whatever timeframe you feel you need. Enjoy your presence. Go outside and see all the life that is around you. Feel those sunrays (natural vitamin D is good for you) and the breeze, hear the birds singing their songs and even the plane flying hundreds of miles above you. Live in the now. It is OK to post pictures and videos on social media, but that is not your life. That is just a small piece of what you want to share. Make memories; allow your memories to be your camera roll. More times than not, people always have their phones in their hands and don't even enjoy the now, what, and who around them. Let's start living in the now.

Notes, Ideas, Thoughts

Seek to be whole, not perfect.

—Oprah

CHAPTER 12

Escape

By moving forward, we want to change what we listen to as well. We imitate or conform to what we surround ourselves with. Have you ever met someone, and they had this phrase or statement they always said, and you found yourself saying it? Right; yes, I do as well. We pick up and adapt to what we surround ourselves with. This is both positive and negative.

Music is also powerful. Research has verified that listening to music can reduce blood pressure and anxiety and improve sleep, mental alertness, and even memory. Music can in fact change our mood. So, if I want my mood changed, I will prefer it to be changed in a positive light.

Did you ever play any sports in school? If so, remember when you came out to the court, when they played music? When a boxer comes out and walks down that aisle, they are playing their music. In the locker room where everyone is chanting, the music is hyping them up, getting their adrenaline running; their hearts are beating, and they are hyped and ready to play the game. You are about to run your one-hundred-meter sprint, and you are in the slumps. Do you think you are going to give it your all? Are you going to win? But I guarantee you that even if an unfavorable event took place before, if you put in your AirPods and bump that one song that just does it for you, you will be ready on those blocks to smoke everyone out.

List a few songs that you know put you in an inspirational mood—a mood that puts a smile on your face, a mood that makes you want to keep persevering, makes you laugh, or has sentimental meaning. If you don't think you have any, search some songs up with the great invention of Google.

Songs

______________________ ______________________

______________________ ______________________

______________________ ______________________

______________________ ______________________

______________________ ______________________

______________________ ______________________

We have so many apps that can assist with motivation, inspiration, laughter, and so much more. Try out some podcasts or motivational apps. I listen to motivational podcasts, and I have an app called "I Am." It has inspirational quotes that are sent to your phone every few hours; it is nice to see. I also have a dictionary app. It sends me new words four times a day. Nothing wrong with expanding your vocabulary.

So, below, research some podcasts that you find interesting and jot them down, along with some self-help apps and books. You can find some good free ones.

Podcasts	**Apps**
____________________	____________________
____________________	____________________
____________________	____________________
____________________	____________________
____________________	____________________
____________________	____________________
____________________	____________________

Books

____________________ ____________________

____________________ ____________________

____________________ ____________________

____________________ ____________________

Music was my refuge. I could crawl into the space between the notes and curl my back to loneliness.

—Maya Angelou

As we start the twenty-one-day journaling process, you will find that after the seventh day, there will be an entry for your date, so start planning your dates in advance. Your dates do not have to consist of always spending money. But for the journaling purpose of the twenty-one days, you should have gone on a date with you a total of four times; if you are able to do more, go for it. But it is suggested that you take yourself out at least once a month. You work hard; you are deserving of treating yourself. As you write, stray away from negative writing. Keep it optimistic and uplifting. Write down goals and steps to take to get there. We are improving you for you and eventually for others who enter your life.

Notes, Ideas, Thoughts

Dating yourself is a lifelong relationship.

—Unknown

CHAPTER 13

Journaling

Day 1

You can be happy and still want to improve. You can be happy and still want to be healthier, smarter, more generous, and more compassionate. Because happiness isn't about complacency. It's about knowing you're enough.

—Unknown

Day 2

A great marriage isn't something that just happens; it's something that must be created.

—Fawn Weaver

No More Excuses...*it's time to be HER!*

Day 3

But blessed is the one who trusts in the Lord,
whose confidence is in him.

—Jeremiah 17:7

No More Excuses...*it's time to be HER!*

Day 4

Self-care is never a selfish act—it is simply good stewardship of the only gift I have, the gift I was put on earth to offer to others.

—Parker Palmer

No More Excuses...*it's time to be HER!*

Day 5

One of the greatest regrets in life is being what others would want you to be rather than being yourself.

—Shannon L. Alder

No More Excuses...*it's time to be HER!*

Day 6

It's all about falling in love with yourself and sharing that love with someone who appreciates you, rather than looking for love to compensate for a self-love deficit.

—Eartha Kitt

No More Excuses...*it's time to be HER!*

Day 7

It is interesting how often we can't see all the ways in which we are being strong.

—Lena Dunham

Date Experience #2

Like your first date, revisit what you wrote. Is there anything you would change? Compare it to your previous dating experience. Were you more relaxed? Did you find that you were more in tune with yourself? Did you find out that you really don't enjoy doing something like you thought you did when you were out with others? How have things changed?

It is interesting how often we can't see all the ways in which we are being strong.

—Lena Dunham

Day 8

Self-love is an ocean, and your heart is a vessel. Make it full, and any excess will spill over into the lives of the people you hold dear. But you must come first.

—Beau Taplin

Day 9

I took a deep breath and listened to the old brag of my heart. I am, I am, I am.

—Sylvia Plath

No More Excuses...*it's time to be HER!*

Day 10

A man cannot be comfortable without his own approval.

—Mark Twain

Day 11

Your self-worth is determined by you. You don't have to depend on someone telling you who you are.

—Beyoncé

Day 12

Once you've accepted your flaws, no one can use them against you.

—George R. R. Martin

Day 13

The hardest challenge is to be yourself in a world where everyone is trying to make you be somebody else.

—E. E. Cummings

No More Excuses...*it's time to be HER!*

Day 14

Rock bottom became the solid foundation on which I rebuilt my life.

—J. K. Rowling

Date Experience #3

Reread what you wrote. Is there anything you would change? Compare it to your other two dating experiences. Were you feeling stress-free? Did you find that you were more in tune with yourself? Did you find out anything new about yourself? How will you incorporate this into your daily life?

To love oneself is the beginning of a lifelong romance.

—Oscar Wilde

Day 15

And you? When will you begin that long journey into yourself

—Rumi

No More Excuses...*it's time to be HER!*

Day 16

My mission, should I choose to accept it, is to find peace with exactly who and what I am. To take pride in my thoughts, my appearance, my talents, my flaws and to stop this incessant worrying that I can't be loved as I am.

—Anaïs Nin

No More Excuses...*it's time to be HER!*

Day 17

There is you and you. This is a relationship. This is the most important relationship.

—Nayyirah Waheed

Day 18

I must undertake to love myself and to respect myself as though my very life depends upon self-love and self-respect.

—Maya Angelou

No More Excuses...*it's time to be HER!*

Day 19

When you take care of yourself, you're a better person for others. When you feel good about yourself, you treat others better.

—William Shakespeare

No More Excuses...*it's time to be HER!*

Day 20

If you have no confidence in self, you are twice defeated in the race of life.

—Marcus Garvey

No More Excuses...*it's time to be HER!*

Day 21

For me, self-love is like, "Am I sleeping enough? Eating well?" Not, "Am I eating well to be able to fit into my skinny jeans?" but, "Am I eating well to be healthy and strong?" And to acknowledge the good, because there is always a lot of good.

—Kerry Washington

Date Experience #4

This will be your last dating experience for this journal. Please don't stop here. Keep going, keep treating yourself, keep loving on you, and by doing this, you are teaching others how to love you and your expectations. With this date, was there anything you would change? Did you find yourself not looking around so much to see if people were watching you? Even if your answer is no, that's OK; as time passes, you won't even notice the people around you. Compare it to your other three dating experiences. By this time, have you found something new within you? Let's hear it.

____

____

____

____

____

You are beaming at this point, doing things you never would have thought you would do alone. You are on the right track of discovering you, loving you, appreciating you and your time. Time is such an amazing gift. When you make plans and you give someone your time, this speaks volumes; you are saying, "You are important enough to me that I am willing to shut everyone and everything else off and spend it only with you," and time is something that we never get back, no matter how hard we try.

The two most powerful warriors are patience and time.

—Leo Tolstoy

No More Excuses...*it's time to be HER!*

CHAPTER 14

What's Next?

You have completed your twenty-one days of journaling. I encourage you to continue to journal. You don't need to go out and buy a $1,000 journal; go to your local store and purchase a spiral notebook, whatever you want. I have a notepad on my phone that I pull out to jot down some ideas. You don't have to break the bank or find something fancy; this is for you, by you, to you.

I started this journal for me in the beginning to straighten out all these thoughts and emotions that were going through my head and to put them in their correct places, but as I continued to write, I saw that this could help more than just me, inspire more than just me, and encourage more than just me.

You are important; you are valued, enough, and loved. There is nothing wrong with making yourself proud. To step out on faith to do what you were dreaming about doing, it is time to get ahold of your emotions, get rid of negative thinking, and move past anxiety, overthinking, and depression—to forgive yourself for your past and persevere toward a brighter future that, yes, you deserve.

My prayer is that this will inspire you to see yourself, the authentic you, and everything that comes along with you. You are unique; there is no one out there like you, and this is your power. Surround yourself with like-minded people. I encourage you to read more about your passion, do research, and find ways to establish your visions, goals, and dreams into reality.

Don't stop talking to yourself. Remember, I gave myself a whole pep talk before I walked through that door, and no one knew the difference. True happiness comes from within. The people that you allow in your circle are there to accompany your happiness; it is not their job to make you happy.

Some people, at the end of the year, would book a hotel room for the weekend and plan their next year. They would plan trips and dates with their friends. This lady would send a questionnaire to her closest friends to fill out. I personally do not think that is a bad idea; this may be extreme to some, but others may have more of a time crunch. I know I am one who needs to plan out in advance. I love spontaneous things, but sometimes they just don't work out without planning.

To find yourself, think for yourself.

—Socrates

Your Final Thoughts

At the end of the day, you are in control of your own happiness. Life is going to happen whether you overthink it, overstress it, or not. Just experience life and be happy along the way. You can't control everything in your life, but you can control your happiness.

—Holly Holm

CHAPTER 15

"Phenomenal Woman"

Pretty women wonder where
    my secret lies.
I'm not cute or built to suit a
    fashion model's size
But when I start to tell them,
They think I'm telling lies.
I say,
It's in the reach of my arms,
The span of my hips,
The stride of my step,
The curl of my lips.
I'm a woman
Phenomenally.
Phenomenal woman,
That's me.

I walk into a room
Just as cool as you please,
And to a man,
The fellows stand or
Fall down on their knees.
Then they swarm around me,
A hive of honey bees.
I say,
It's the fire in my eyes,
And the flash of my teeth,
The swing in my waist,
And the joy in my feet.
I'm a woman
Phenomenally.

Phenomenal woman,
That's me.

Men themselves
have wondered
What they see in me.

That's me.

I walk into a room
Just as cool as you please,
And to a man,
The fellows stand or
Fall down on their knees.
Then they swarm around me,
A hive of honey bees.

The grace of my style.
I'm a woman
Phenomenally.
Phenomenal woman,
That's me.

Now you understand
Just why my head's not bowed.
I don't shout or jump about
Or have to talk real loud.
When you see me passing,
It ought to make you proud.

They try so much
But they can't touch
My inner mystery.
When I try to show them,
They say they still can't see.
I say,
It's in the arch of my back,
The sun of my smile,
The ride of my breasts,

I say,
It's in the click of my heels,
The bend of my hair,
the palm of my hand,
The need for my care.
'Cause I'm a woman
Phenomenally.
Phenomenal woman,
That's me.

—Maya Angelou

How to connect with the author:

@jojo.a.scott

@aboutjojo_jas

jojo-a-scott

jojo.a.scott

www.aboutjojo.com

ABOUT THE AUTHOR

Jo "Jojo" Scott was born in Connecticut and raised in Florida where she still resides. A widow and single mother of four children, Jo wants to live as an example to her children and other women. She is currently working on her 3rd degree. Her passions include reading, lifting weights, and exploring classy new environments around Florida. She loves God and wants her children to know that no matter how hard life gets, if you never give up you can see things change.

Milton Keynes UK
Ingram Content Group UK Ltd.
UKHW021110200524
442968UK00015B/1050